A FARAWAY TREE

Adventure

The Land of
GOODIES

EGMONT

The World of the
FARAWAY TREE

MOON-FACE lives at the very top. In his house is the start of THE SLIPPERY-SLIP, a huge slide that curves all the way down inside the trunk of the tree.

SILKY lives below Moon-Face. She is the prettiest little fairy you ever did see.

SAUCEPAN MAN is a funny old thing. His saucepans make lots of noise when they jangle together, so he can't hear very well.

CHAPTER ONE
The Woodpecker Brings a Note

Joe, Beth, Frannie and Rick were usually very good children, but they had been **rather naughty lately.** Rick and Joe quarrelled, and they fell over when they began to wrestle with one another, and broke a little table.

Then Beth **scorched** a tablecloth when she was ironing it — and Frannie tore a hole in her clothes when she went picking blackberries.

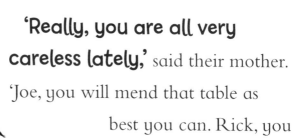

'Really, you are all very careless lately,' said their mother. 'Joe, you will mend that table as best you can. Rick, you must help him — and if I see you quarrelling like that again I shall send you both to bed at once. Frannie, why didn't you put on your old clothes when you went to pick blackberries, as I told you to? Now you will have to mend your clothes, and properly.'

Beth had to wash the tablecloth carefully to try and get the scorch marks out of it.

'**Oh my,** it's a pity all these things have happened this week,' groaned Joe to Rick, as the two boys did their best  to mend the table. **'I'm afraid the Land of Goodies will come and go before we get there!** I daren't ask Mother or Father if we can go off to the Faraway Tree. We've been so careless that they are sure to say no.'

'Moon-Face and the others will be wondering why we don't go,' said Beth, almost in tears.

3

They were. The Land of Goodies had come, and a **delicious** smell kept coming down the ladder. Moon-Face waited and waited for the children to come, but they didn't.

Then he heard that the Land of Goodies was going to move away the next afternoon, and he wondered what to do.

'We said we'd wait for the children – but we don't want to miss going ourselves,' he said to Silky. **'We had better send a note to them.** Perhaps something has happened to stop them coming.'

So they wrote a note, and went down to
ask the Owl to take it. **But he was asleep.**
So they went to the woodpecker, who had
a hole in the tree for himself, and he said he
would take it.

He flew off with it in his beak. He soon
found the cottage and tapped on the window
with his beak.

'A lovely **woodpecker!**' cried Joe,
looking up. 'See the red on his head? He's got
a note for us!'

He opened the window. Mother was there, in the same room as the children, and she looked surprised to see such an **unexpected visitor.**

Joe took the note. The bird stayed on the windowsill, waiting for an answer.

7

Joe read it and then showed it to the others. They all looked rather sad. **It was dreadful** to know that the lovely Land of Goodies had come and was going so soon – and they couldn't visit it.

'**Tell Moon-Face we've been in trouble and can't come,**' said Joe.

The bird spread its wings, but Mother looked up and spoke.

'**Wait a minute!**' she said to the bird. Then she turned to Joe. 'Read me the note,' she said.

Joe read it out loud:

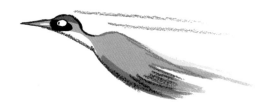

'**The Land of Goodies!**' said Mother in amazement. 'Well, I never did hear of such funny happenings! I suppose there are lots of nice things to eat there, and that's why you all want to go. Well – you have been in trouble lately – but you've done your best to put things right. You can go tomorrow morning!'

'**Mother! Oh, Mother, thank you!**' cried the children.

'**Thank you, Aunt Polly!**' said Rick, hugging her. 'Oh, how lovely!'

'Tell Moon-Face we'll come as soon as we can tomorrow morning,' said Joe to the listening woodpecker. He nodded his red-splashed head and flew off.

CHAPTER TWO
Up to the Land of Goodies

The children talked together, excited.

'I won't have any breakfast,' said Beth. 'It's not much good going to the Land of Goodies unless we're hungry!'

'That's a good idea,' said Rick. 'I think I won't have any supper tonight either!'

So when the time came for the four children to set off to the Enchanted Wood, they were **terribly hungry!**

They ran to the Faraway Tree and climbed up it in excitement.

'I hope there are doughnuts,' said Joe.

'I want chocolate mousse,' said Beth.

'I can't begin to say the things I'd like,' said greedy Rick.

'Well, don't,' said Joe. 'Save your breath and hurry. You're being left behind!'

13

14

They got to Moon-Face's, and **shouted loudly** to him. He came running out of his tree-house in delight.

'**Oh, good, good!**' he cried. 'You are nice and early. **Silky, they're here!** Go down and call old Saucepan. He's with Mister Watzisname. I'm sure Saucepan would like to come too.'

It wasn't long before **seven excited people** were climbing up the ladder to the Land of Goodies. How they longed to see what it was like!

Well, it was much better than anyone imagined!

It was a small place, set with little crooked houses and shops – and every house and shop was made from things to eat! The first house that the children saw was amazing.

'Look at that house!' cried Joe. 'Its walls are made of **sugar** – and the

chimneys are **chocolate** – and the window sills are **peppermint cream!**'

'And look at that shop!' cried Rick. 'It's got walls made of **chocolate,** and the door is made of **marzipan.** And I'm sure the windowsills are **gingerbread!**'

The Land of Goodies was really a very extraordinary place. Everything in it seemed to be eatable. And then the children caught sight of the trees and bushes and called out in surprise:

'Look! That tree is growing muffins!'

'And that one has got buds that are opening out into cakes! **It's a Cake Tree!**'

'And look at this little tree here – it's growing **big, flat, white flowers** like plates – and the middle of the flowers is full of ice-cream. **Let's taste it.**'

They tasted it – and it was ice-cream!

22

There was another small bush that grew clusters of a **curious-looking fruit,** like flat berries of all colours – and, will you believe it, when the children picked the fruit it was really **little lollipops,** all neatly growing together like a bunch of grapes.

'Ooh, lovely!' said Joe, who liked lollipops very much. 'Gosh, look at that white fence over there – surely it isn't made of marshmallow!'

It was. The children tore off pieces from the fence, and **munched** the marshmallow. It was the nicest they had ever tasted.

The shops were full of things to eat.
You should have seen them! Joe felt as if
he would like a hot dog and he went into a
hot dog shop. The rolls were tumbling one
by one out of a machine.

The handle was being turned by an
odd-looking person. He was flat and

golden brown, and had raisin-like eyes.

'I think he is a gingerbread man!'
whispered Joe to the others. 'He's just like
the gingerbread people that Mother makes
for us.'

The children chose a hot dog each and
went out, munching.

They wandered into the next shop. It had lovely big cakes, set out in rows. Some were yellow, some were pink, and some white.

'Your name, please?' asked the funny little woman there, looking at Beth, who had asked for a cake.

'**Beth,**' said the little girl in surprise. And there in the middle of the cake her name appeared in pink sugar letters!

Of course, **all the others wanted cakes, too,** then, just to see their names come!

29

'We shall never be able to eat all these,' said
Moon-Face, looking at the seven cakes that
had suddenly appeared. But, you know, they
tasted **so delicious** that it wasn't very
long before they all went!

CHAPTER THREE

Rick Gets into Trouble

Into shop after shop went the children and the others, tasting everything they could see. They had tomato soup, poached eggs, ginger buns, chocolate fingers, ice-creams, and **goodness knows** what else.

'Well, I just CAN'T eat anything more,' said Silky at last. 'I've been really greedy. I am sure I'll be ill if I eat anything else.'

'Oh, Silky!' said Rick. 'Don't stop. I can go on for quite a long time yet.'

'Rick, you're greedy, really greedy,' said Joe. 'You ought to stop.'

'Well, I'm not going to,' said Rick. The others looked at him.

'You're getting very fat,' said Joe suddenly. 'You won't be able to get down the hole! **You be careful, Rick.** You're not to go into any more shops.'

'All right,' said Rick, looking sulky.

But although he did not go into the shops, **can you guess what he did?** He broke off some of a gingerbread windowsill – and then he took a knocker from a door. It was made of peppermint, and Rick sucked it in delight.

The others had not seen him do these things – but the man whose knocker Rick had pulled off did see him! **He opened his door and came running out.**

'**Hey, hey!**' he cried angrily. 'Bring back my knocker at once! You bad, naughty boy!'

When Joe and the others heard the angry voice behind them, they turned in surprise. Nobody but Rick knew what the angry little man was talking about.

'Knocker?' said Joe, in amazement. 'What knocker? We haven't got your knocker.'

'That bad boy is eating my knocker!' cried the man, and he pointed to Rick. 'I had a beautiful one, made of **lovely peppermint** – and now that boy has nearly eaten it all up!'

They all stared at Rick. He went very
red. What was left of the knocker was in his
mouth.

'Did you really take his peppermint
knocker?' said Joe, glaring at Rick.
'Whatever were you thinking of, Rick?'

'Well, I just never thought,' said Rick, swallowing the rest of the knocker in a hurry. 'I saw it there on the door – and it looked so nice. **I'm very sorry.**'

'That's all very well,' said the angry man. 'But being sorry won't bring back my knocker. You're a bad boy. You come and sit in my house till the others are ready to go. I won't have you going about in our land eating knockers and chimneys and windowsills!'

'You'd better go, Rick,' said Joe. 'We'll call for you when we're ready to go home. We won't be long now. Anyway, you've eaten quite enough.'

So poor Rick had to go into the house with the angry little man, who made him sit on a stool and keep still. The others wandered off again.

'We mustn't be here much longer,' said Moon-Face. 'It's almost time for this land to move on. **Look! Strawberries and cream.'**

The children stared at the strawberries and cream. They had never seen such a strange sight before.

The strawberries grew by the hundred on strawberry plants – but each strawberry had its own **big blob of cream** growing on it, ready to be eaten.

'They are even sugared!' said Joe, picking one. 'Look – my strawberry is powdered with white sugar – and, **oh, the cream is delicious!'**

They enjoyed the strawberries and cream, and then Joe had a good idea.

'**I know! What about taking some of these lovely goodies back with us?**' he said. 'Watzisname would love a plum pie – and the Angry Pixie would like some of those ice-cream flowers – and Dame Washalot would like some strawberries.'

'And Mother would like lots of things, too,' said Beth happily.

So they began collecting puddings and pies and cakes. It was fun. The cherry pie had so many cherries that they dripped all down Moon-Face's leg.

'You'll have to take a bath later, Moon-Face,' said Silky. 'You're very sticky.'

They nearly forgot to call for poor Rick. As they passed the house whose knocker he had eaten, he **banged loudly** on the window, and they all stopped.

'**Gosh!** We nearly forgot about Rick!' said Beth. '**Rick, Rick, come on! We're going!**'

Rick came running out of the house. The little man called after him: 'Now, don't you eat anybody's knocker again!'

'Goodness! Why have you got all those things?' asked Rick in surprise, looking at the puddings and pies and cakes. 'Are they for our supper?'

'Rick! How can you think of supper after eating such a lot!' cried Joe. 'Well, I'm sure I couldn't even eat a piece of chocolate before tomorrow morning. **No - these things are for Watzisname and Dame Washalot and Mother. Come on.** Moon-Face says this land will soon be on the move.'

They all went to the hole that led down through the cloud. It didn't take long to climb down the ladder and on to the big branch outside Moon-Face's house.

49

Rick came last – and he suddenly missed his footing and **fell right down the ladder** on the top of the others below. And he knocked the **puddings, pies and cakes** right out of their hands!

Down went all the goodies, **bumping** from branch to branch. The children and the others stared after them in dismay.

Then there came a very angry yell from below. **'Who's thrown a cherry pie at me?** Wait till I get them. I've got cherries and syrup all over me. **It burst on my head. Oh, oh!'**

Then there came an angry
shout from lower down still.
**'Plum pie! Plum pie in
my wash-tub!** Hot dogs in
my wash-tub! Peppermints
down my neck! Oh, you rascals
up there – I'm coming up after
you, yes I am!'

And from still lower down
came the voice of the Angry
Pixie – and a very angry
pixie he was indeed!

'Ice-cream on my nose!
Ice-cream down my neck!
Ice-cream in my pockets!
What next? Who's doing
all this? Wait till I come up
and tell them what I think!'

The children listened, half frightened
and very amused. They began to giggle.

'**Plum pie in Dame Washalot's tub!**'
giggled Joe.

'**Ice-cream on the Angry Pixie's nose!**'
said Beth.

'**Look out,** I believe they really are coming up!' said Joe, in alarm. '**Look - isn't that Watzisname?**'

57

They all peered down the tree.

Yes – it was Watzisname climbing up, looking very angry. The Saucepan Man leaned over a bit too far, and nearly fell. Rick just caught him in time – but one of his kettles came loose and fell down.

It bounced from branch to branch and landed on poor old Watzisname's big head!

He gave a **tremendous** yell.

'What! Is it you, Saucepan, throwing all these things down the tree? What you want is a good scolding. And you'll get it! And anybody else up there playing tricks will get a fine scolding, too!'

'A scolding!' said Dame Washalot's voice. **'A SCOLDING!'** roared the Angry Pixie not far behind.

CHAPTER FIVE
Moon-Face Gets a Scolding

'Gosh!' said Joe in alarm. 'It looks as if the Land of Scoldings is about to arrive up here. I vote we go home. You'd better shut your door, Moon-Face, and you and Silky and Saucepan had better lie down on the sofa and the bed and pretend to be asleep. Then maybe those angry people will think it's somebody up in the Land of Goodies that has been throwing all those things down.'

'Rick ought to stay up there and get the scoldings,' said Moon-Face gloomily. 'First he goes and eats somebody's door knocker and gets into trouble. Then he falls on top of us all and sends all the goodies down the tree.'

'I'm going down the slippery-slip with the children,' said Silky, who was afraid of Mister Watzisname when he was in a temper.

'I can climb up to my house and lock myself in before all those angry people come down again. **Saucepan, why don't you come too?'**

Saucepan thought he would. **So the children and Silky and Saucepan all slid down the slippery-slip.**

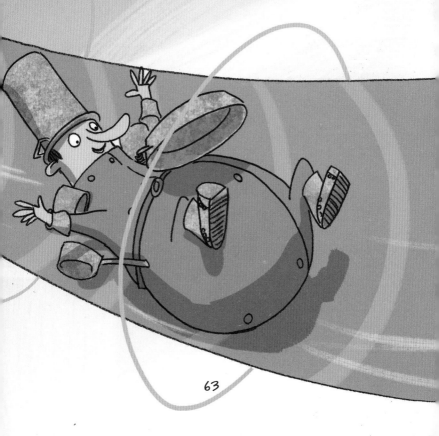

Just in time, too - for Mister Watzisname came shouting up to Moon-Face's door as Joe, who was last, slid down.

Moon-Face had shut his door. He was lying on his bed, pretending to be asleep. Watzisname banged hard on the door.

Moon-Face didn't answer.

Watzisname peeped in at the window.

'Moon-Face! **Wake up!** Wake up, I say!'

'What's the matter?' said Moon-Face, in a
sleepy voice, sitting up and rubbing his eyes.

Dame Washalot and the Angry Pixie came up, too. The Pixie had ice-cream all over him, and Watzisname had cherry pie down him. **They were all very angry.**

They opened Moon-Face's door
and went in.

'Who was it that threw all those things
down on us?' asked Watzisname. 'Where's
Saucepan? Did he throw that kettle?
I'm going to **scold** him.'

'Whatever are you talking about?' said Moon-Face, pretending not to know. 'How sticky you are, Watzisname!'

'And so are you!' yelled Watzisname, suddenly, seeing cherry syrup shining all down Moon-Face's legs. 'It was you who threw that pudding down on me! **My, oh my, I'll give you such a scolding!'**

Then all three of them went for poor
Moon-Face, who got a terrible scolding.
**He rolled over to the slippery-slip,
and slid down it in a fright.**

He shot out of the trapdoor just in time to
see Silky and Saucepan saying goodbye to the
children. They were **very surprised** when
Moon-Face shot out beside them.

'**I've had a scolding!**' wept Moon-Face. 'They all scolded me because I was sticky, so they thought I'd thrown all the goodies at them. And now I'm afraid to go back because they will be waiting for me.'

'**Poor Moon-Face,**' said Joe. 'And it was all Rick's fault. Listen: Silky can climb back to her house.

But you and Saucepan had better come back with us and stay the night. Rick and I will sleep downstairs on the sofa, and you can have our beds. Mother won't mind.'

'**All right,**' said Moon-Face, wiping his eyes. '**That will be fun.** Oh, what a pity we wasted all those lovely, goodies! I really do think Rick is a clumsy boy!'

They all went home together, and poor Rick didn't say a word. **But he did wish he could make up for all he had done!**